CW01084933

CONTENTS

CATHOLIC

PRAYERS

PREFACE

This new edition of the *Book of Catholic Prayers* by Sol y Tierra products is a complete prayer resource for Catholics.

In this new 2022 edition, the reader will find a bigger format for easy reading, beautiful daily prayers and a selection of Psalms to celebrate the joy of living a Christian life.

The intent of this book is to enhance the practice of praying at home and the participation in the Mass, deepening into the experience of receiving the Sacraments, intensifying the celebration of the Mysteries of Salvation, and encouraging more knowledgeable and confident prayer throughout the liturgical year.

With a higher quality cover, this *Book of Catholic Prayers* is designed to strengthen the bond between those who pray with and God.

The Book of Catholic Prayers incorporates dozens of favorite Catholic prayers in a very readable format.

ACKNOWLEDGMENTS

Writing a book is harder than I thought and more rewarding than I could have ever imagined. None of this would have been possible without the inspiration given by my parents. In life, They were my mentors, through them, I discovered the pwer of praying and the hugue impact that Faith makes every day.

A very special thanks to my family. To my three children, Bernat, Roser, and Pere; they keep me motivated to go deeper in my heart, where I find the force to write books about prayers and meditations. To my siblings, Jaume, M Julia, and Jordi, whos presence brings me the fulfilment of living the family life.

And I'm grateful for you, the reader. The world is a better place thanks to people like you, taking time off, and to dedicate it to pray and to practice devotions to God.

CATEGORIES

Categories of prayers included in this title are:

- The Mass - Our Greatest Prayer
- Daily Prayers
- Morning Prayers
- Night Prayers
- Confession Prayers
- Prayers Before Communion
- Prayers After Communion
- Prayers for Liturgical Times
- Prayers to Our Blessed Mother
- Prayers from the Psalms
- Prayers for special requests
- Prayers of the Rosary
- Beautiful Psalms for daily joy

THE HOLY MASS

THE GREATEST PRAYER

The Holy Mass is our most cherissed moment of connection with God. Use the following section to follow the Mass. This is also useful if following the Mass at distance, on the TV or on the radio.

ESSENCE OF THE MASS

"At the Last Supper, our Saviour instituted the Eucharistic sacrifice of His Body and Blood. He did this in order to perpetuate the sacrifice of the Cross throughout the centuries until He should come again.

Thus the Mass is:

• the true sacrifice of the New Covenant, in which a holy and living Victim is offered, Jesus Christ, and we in union with Him, as a gift of love and obedience to the Father;

• a sacred meal and spiritual banquet of the children of God;

• a paschal meal, which evokes the passage (passover) of Jesus from this world to the Father; it renders Him present and makes Him live again in souls, and anticipates our passage to the Kingdom of God;

• a COMMUNITARIAN MEAL, that is, a gathering together of the Head and His members, of Jesus and His Church, His Mystical

Body, in order to carry out a perfect Divine worship.

Thus, the Mass is the greatest prayer we have. Through it we give thanks and praise to the Father for the wonderful future He has given us in His Son. We also ask forgiveness for our sins and beg the Father's blessing upon us and all human beings.

STRUCTURE OF THE HOURS OF THE MASS

INTRODUCTORY RITES

The Eucharist consists of the Liturgy of the Word and the Liturgy of the Eucharist plus introductory and concluding rites. During the Introductory Rites acts of prayer and penitence prepare us to meet Christ as He comes in Word and Sacrament. We gather as a worshipping community to celebrate our unity with and in Him.

LITURGY OF THE WORD

The proclamation of God's Word is always centred on Christ. Jesus is the Word of God Himself and the Author of Revelation. It is He Himself Who speaks to us when the Sacred Scriptures are liturgically proclaimed, and He calls for our positive response.

LITURGY OF THE EUCHARIST

We enter now into the Eucharistic sacrifice itself, the Supper of the Lord. We are God's new people, the redeemed brothers and sisters of Christ, gathered around His table.

PREPARATION OF THE GIFTS

We bring forward our gifts of bread and wine as well as our monetary offerings for the upkeep of the church building and the clergy, and the relief of the poor. These are but a symbol of our inner readiness to give God all of ourselves with our hopes and disappointments, our work and leisure, and our whole everyday lives.

EUCHARISTIC PRAYER

The Eucharistic service of praise and thanksgiving is the centre of the celebration. We join Christ in His sacrifice, celebrating His memorial and acknowledging the wonderful works of God in our lives. At the consecration of the bread and wine Christ's words spoken through the priest accomplish what they signify: His Eucharistic Body and Blood, His Real Presence with all the riches of the Kingdom.

The people now praise Christ in the Memorial Acclamation. We celebrate the fact that Christ has redeemed us, is with us now to apply that Redemption to each of us, and will return in glory to perfect that Redemption for all.

COMMUNION RITE

The Communion Rite is the conclusion of the Mass. It is the part when God gives a gift to us after we have presented our gift to Him: Jesus Christ, the Son of God and Saviour of the world. We receive the Body and Blood, Soul and Divinity of Jesus Christ, the

Bread of Life, that gives access to eternity.

CONCLUDING RITE

We have heard God's Word and responded to it. We have received Christ's Body and Blood and achieved greater union with Him and others. Now we leave to praise and bless the Lord in our daily lives."

COMMON PRAYERS

Common Prayers are good to establish the connection between our selves and the Holy Spirit. Read the following prayers in a meditative tone, to enhance calm and joy.

Sign of the Cross

In the name of the Father, and of the Son,
and of the Holy Spirit.
Amen.

The Apostles' Creed

I believe in God, the Father almighty, creator of heaven and earth.
I believe in Jesus Christ, His only Son, our Lord.

He was conceived by the power of the Holy Spirit and born of the Virgin Mary.

He suffered under Pontius Pilate, was crucified, died, and was buried.

He descended to the dead.

On the third day, he rose again.

He ascended into heaven and is seated at the right hand of the Father.

He will come again to judge the living and the dead.

I believe in the Holy Spirit, the holy catholic Church, the communion of saints, the forgiveness of sins, the resurrection of the body, and the life everlasting.
Amen.

Our Father

Our Father, who art in heaven, hallowed be Thy name; Thy kingdom comes; Thy will be done on earth as it is in heaven. Give us this day our daily bread, and forgive us our trespasses as we forgive those who trespass against us; and lead us not into temptation, but deliver us from evil.
Amen.

Hail Mary

Hail Mary, full of grace! The Lord is with thee. Blessed art thou among women and blessed is the fruit of thy womb, Jesus. Holy Mary, Mother of God, pray for us sinners, now and at the hour of our death.
Amen.

Doxology

Glory be to the Father, and to the Son, and to the Holy Spirit. As it was in the beginning, is now and ever shall be, world without end.
Amen.

An Act of Faith

O my God, I firmly believe that You are one God in three divine persons, Father, Son, and Holy Spirit. I believe that Your divine Son became man and died for our sins and that he will come to judge the living and the dead.

I believe these and all the truths which the holy Catholic Church teaches because You have revealed them, who can neither deceive nor be deceived.
Amen.

An Act of Hope

O my God, trusting in Your promises and because You are faithful, powerful, and merciful, I hope, through the merits of Jesus Christ, for the pardon of my sins, final perseverance, and the blessed glory of heaven.

An Act of Love

O my God, because You are infinite goodness and worthy of infinite love, I love You with my whole heart above all things, and for love of You I love my neighbor as myself.

I forgive all who have offended me and ask pardon of all whom I have offended. Amen

An Act of Contrition

O my God, I am heartily sorry for having offended Thee and I detest all my sins because I dread the loss of heaven and the pains of hell; but most of all because they offend Thee, my God, Who are all good and deserving of all my love.

I firmly resolve, with the help of Thy grace, to confess my sins, to do penance, and to amend my life. Amen.

Morning Offering

O Jesus, through the Immaculate Heart of Mary, I offer You my prayers, works, joys, and sufferings of this day in union with the Holy Sacrifice of the Mass throughout the world.

I offer them for all the intentions of the Sacred Heart: the salvation of souls, reparation for sin, the reunion of all Christians, and the intentions of our Holy Father, the Pope. Amen.

Prayer in the Morning

Blessed be the Lord, the God of Israel; He has come to His people and set them free.

He has raised up us a mighty savior, born of the house of His servant David.

Through His holy prophets, he promised of old that he would save us from our enemies, from the hands of all who hate us. He promised to show mercy to our fathers and to remember His holy covenant.

This was the oath he swore to our father Abraham: to set us free from the hands of our enemies, free to worship him without fear, holy and righteous in His sight all the days of our life. You, my child, shall be called the prophet of the Most High; for You will go before the Lord to prepare His way, to give His people knowledge of salvation by the forgiveness of their sins. In the tender compassion of our God, the dawn from on high shall break upon us, to shine on those who dwell in darkness and the shadow of death, and to guide our feet into the way of peace. (Luke 1:68-79)

Prayer in the Evening

My soul proclaims the greatness of the Lord, my spirit rejoices in God my Savior; for he has looked with favor on His lowly servant.

From this day all generations will call me blessed: the Almighty has done great things for me, and holy is His Name. He has mercy on those who fear Him in every generation. He has shown the strength of His arm, he has scattered the proud in their conceit.

He has cast down the mighty from their thrones and has lifted up the lowly. He has filled the hungry with good things, and the rich he has sent away empty.

He has come to the help of His servant Israel for He has remembered His promise of mercy, the promise He made to our fathers, to Abraham and His children forever.

(Luke 1:46-55) O eternal God and Ruler of all creation, You have allowed me to reach this hour. Forgive the sins I have committed this day by word, deed or thought.

Purify me, O Lord, from every spiritual and physical stain. Grant that I may rise from this sleep to glorify You by my deeds throughout my entire lifetime, and that I be victorious over every spiritual and physical enemy.

Deliver me, O Lord, from all vain thoughts and from evil desires, for yours is the kingdom and the power, and the glory, Father, Son, and Holy Spirit, now and ever, and forever.
Amen.

Prayer at Night

O my God, I thank You for having preserved me today and for having given me so many blessings and graces.

I renew my dedication to You and ask Your pardon for all my sins.

(review the day quietly then pray The Canticle of Simeon which follows)

Protect us, Lord, as we stay awake; watch over us as we sleep, that awake we may keep watch with Christ, and asleep, rest in His peace (alleluia).

Lord, now let Your servant go in peace;

according to Your word: for my eyes have seen Your salvation which You have prepared in the presence of all peoples: a light for revelation to the Gentiles and for glory to Your people Israel.

(Luke 2:29–32) Glory be to the Father, and to the Son, and to the Holy Spirit. As it was in the beginning, is now and ever shall be, world without end.

Amen.

Protect us, Lord, as we stay awake;

watch over us as we sleep,

that awake we may keep watch with Christ,

and asleep, rest in His peace (alleluia).

The Divine Praises

Blessed be God.

Blessed be His holy name.

Blessed be Jesus Christ, true God, and true man.

Blessed be the name of Jesus.

Blessed be His most Sacred Heart.

Blessed be His most precious Blood.

Blessed be Jesus in the Most Holy Sacrament of the Altar.

Blessed be the Holy Spirit, the Paraclete.

Blessed be the great Mother of God, Mary most holy.

Blessed be her holy and Immaculate Conception.

Blessed be her glorious Assumption.

Blessed be the name of Mary, Virgin and Mother.

Blessed be Saint Joseph, her most chaste spouse.

Blessed be God in His angels and in His Saints.

Grace Before Meals

Bless us, O Lord, and these
Thy gifts which we are about to receive
from Thy bounty.
Through Christ our Lord.
Amen.

Thanksgiving After Meals

We give Thee thanks, almighty God,
for all Thy gifts, who lives and reigns forever and ever.
Amen.
May the souls of the faithful departed,
through the mercy of God,
rest in peace.
Amen.

Memorare

Remember, O most gracious Virgin Mary,
that never was it known that anyone
who fled to your protection,
implored your help, or sought your intercession,
was left unaided.
Inspired by this confidence,
I fly unto you, O Virgin of virgins, my Mother.
To you do I come, before you I stand, sinful and sorrowful.
O Mother of the Word Incarnate,
despise not my petitions,
but in your mercy, hear and answer me.
Amen.

Glory be to the Father

Glory be to the Father, and to the Son,
and to the Holy Spirit.
As it was in the beginning,
is now, and ever shall be,
world without end.
Amen.

Fatima Prayer

O my Jesus, forgive us our sins,
save us from the fires of hell,
and lead all souls to heaven,
especially those most in need of Thy mercy

PRAYERS OF THE ROSARY

Praying the Rosary is a key ressource to create the connection rapidly. Rosary can be prayed at its full length or partially. Follow the next prayers from your soul, slowly, and let words talk to you.

Hail Holy Queen Hail

Holy Queen, Mother of mercy, our life,

our sweetness, and our hope.

To thee do we cry, poor banished children of Eve.

To thee do we send up our sighs,

mourning and weeping in this valley of tears.

Turn, then, most gracious advocate,

thine eyes of mercy toward us,

and after this, our exile,

show unto us the blessed fruit of thy womb, Jesus.

O clement, O loving, O sweet Virgin Mary.

V. Pray for us, O holy Mother of God.

R. That we may be made worthy of the promises of Christ.

Let us pray.

Almighty and everlasting God,

Who by the working of the Holy Spirit didst prepare both body and soul of the glorious Virgin Mother, Mary,

that she might deserve to be made a worthy dwelling for Thy Son,

grant that we who rejoice in her memory, may,
by her loving intercession, be delivered from present evils and
from lasting death, through the same Christ our Lord.
Amen.

Prayer After the Rosary

O God, whose only-begotten Son, by His life, death, and resurrection, has purchased for us the rewards of eternal life; grant, we beseech Thee, that, meditating upon these mysteries of the Most Holy Rosary of the Blessed Virgin Mary, we may imitate what they contain and obtain what they promise, through the same Christ our Lord.

Amen.
V. May the divine assistance remain always with us.
R. And may the souls of the faithful departed, through the mercy of God,
rest in peace.
Amen.

PRAYING THE MYSTERIES

Joyful Mysteries
(Monday and Saturday, Sunday during Christmas season)

1. The Annunciation - Mary learns from the Angel Gabriel that God wishes her to be the mother of God and humbly accepts. (Luke 1:26-38)

2. The Visitation - Mary goes to visit her cousin Elizabeth and is praised by her as "blessed among women." (Luke 1:39-56)

3. The Nativity - Mary gives birth to Jesus in the stable at Bethlehem. (Luke 2:1-20)

4. The Presentation - Mary and Joseph present Jesus to His Heavenly Father in the Temple of Jerusalem forty days after His birth. (Luke 2:22-39)

5. The Finding In The Temple - After searching for three days, Mary and Joseph find the twelve-year-old Jesus sitting in the Temple discussing the law with the learned doctors. (Luke 2:42-52).

Sorrowful Mysteries
(Tuesday and Friday, Sunday during Lent)

1. Agony In The Garden - The thought of our sins and His com-

ing suffering causes the agonizing Savior to sweat blood. (Luke 22:39-44)

2. The Scourging - Jesus is stripped and unmercifully scourged until His body is one mass of bloody wounds. (Matt. 27:26)

3. Crowning With Thorns - Jesus' claim to kingship is ridiculed by putting a crown of thorns on His head and a reed in His hand. (Matt. 27:28- 31)

4. Carrying Of The Cross - Jesus shoulders His own cross and carries it to the place of crucifixion while Mary follows Him sorrowing. (Luke 23:26- 32)

5. Crucifixion - Jesus is nailed to the cross and dies after three hours of agony witnessed by His Mother. (Matt. 27:3350)

Luminous Mysteries
(Thursday)

1. Baptism In The Jordan - After Jesus was baptized, he came up from the water, and behold, the Heaven was opened for him and He saw the Spirit of God descending like a dove and coming to Him.

And a voice came from Heaven saying:

"This is my beloved Son, with whom I am well pleased." (Mt.3:16-17)

2. Jesus Self-Manifestation at Cana - On the third day there was a wedding in Cana in Galilee, and the mother of Jesus was there.
When the wine ran short Mary said to Him, "They have no wine." Jesus said to her, "Woman, how does your concern affect me? My hour has not yet come." His mother told the servers, "Do whatever He tells you." (John 2:1-11)

3. The Proclamation Of The Kingdom And The Call To Conversion - After John had been arrested, Jesus came to Galilee proclaiming the gospel of God: "This is the time of fulfillment. The kingdom of God is at hand. Repent, and believe in the gospel." (Mark 1:14-15)

4. The Transfiguration - While Jesus was praying His face changed in appearance and His clothing became dazzling white.
And behold two men were conversing with Him, Moses and Elijah, who appeared in glory and spoke of His exodus that He was going to accomplish in Jerusalem." (Luke 9:28-31)

5. Institution of the Eucharist - "I am the living bread that came down from heaven; whoever eats this bread will live forever, and the bread that I will give is my flesh for the life of the world." (John 6:51)

Glorious Mysteries
(Wednesday and Sunday, exception: Christmas and Lent)

1. The Resurrection - Jesus rises from the dead on Easter Sunday,

glorious and immortal, as He has predicted. (Matt. 28:1-7)

2. The Ascension - Jesus ascends into Heaven forty days after His resurrection to sit at the right hand of God the Father. (Luke 24:50-51)

3. Descent of Holy Spirit - Jesus sends the Holy Spirit in the form of fiery tongues on His Apostles and disciples. (Acts 2:2-4)

4. Assumption - Mary's soul returns to God and her glorified body is taken up into heaven and reunited with her soul

5. The Coronation - Mary is crowned as Queen of heaven and earth, Queen of angels and saints.

◆ ◆ ◆

Prayer for Acceptance of Death

Most Sacred Heart of Jesus,
I accept from Your hands whatever kind of death
it may please You to send me this day (night)
with all its pains, penalties, and sorrows;
in reparation for all of my sins,
for the souls in Purgatory,
for all those who will die today
and for Your greater glory.

Amen.

Prayer to the archangel Saint Michael

Saint Michael the Archangel, defend us in battle.
Be our protection against the wickedness and snares of the devil;
May God rebuke him, we humbly pray;
And do thou,
O Prince of the Heavenly Host, by the power of God,
thrust into hell Satan and all evil spirits
who wander through the world for the ruin of souls.
Amen

Sacred Heart of Jesus Prayer

O most holy Heart of Jesus,
fountain of every blessing,
I adore You, I love You,
and with a lively sorrow for my sins,
I offer You this poor heart of mine.
Make me humble, patient, pure,
and wholly obedient to Your will.
Grant, good Jesus, that I may live in You and for You
Amen

Come Holy Ghost

Come Holy Spirit, fill the hearts of your faithful and kindle in them the fire of your love.
Send forth your Spirit and they shall be created.

And You shall renew the face of the earth.
O, God, who by the light of the Holy Spirit,
did instruct the hearts of the faithful,
grant that by the same Holy Spirit
we may be truly wise and
ever enjoy His consolations,
through Christ Our Lord,

Amen.

Angel of God

Angel of God,
my guardian dear,
to whom God's love commits me here,
ever this day be at my side,
to light and guard, to rule and guide.
Amen.

Eternal Rest

Eternal rest grant unto them, O Lord,
and let perpetual light shine upon them.
May they rest in peace.
Amen.

The Angelus

℣. The Angel of the LORD declared unto Mary,

℟. And she conceived of the Holy Spirit.

Hail Mary, full of grace;
the LORD is with thee:
blessed art thou amongst women,
and blessed is the Fruit of thy womb, Jesus.
Holy Mary, Mother of God,
pray for us sinners,
now and at the hour of our death.

℣. Behold the handmaid of the LORD.

℟. Be it done unto me according to thy word.

Hail Mary, full of grace;
the LORD is with thee:
blessed art thou amongst women,
and blessed is the Fruit of thy womb, Jesus.
Holy Mary, Mother of God,
pray for us sinners,
now and at the hour of our death.

℣. And the Word was made flesh.

℟. And dwelt among us.

Hail Mary, full of grace;
the LORD is with thee:
blessed art thou amongst women,
and blessed is the Fruit of thy womb, Jesus.
Holy Mary, Mother of God, pray for us sinners,

now and at the hour of our death.

℣. Pray for us, O Holy Mother of God.

℟. That we may be made worthy of the promises of Christ.

Let us pray,

Pour forth, we beseech Thee, O LORD,
Thy grace into our hearts;
that, we, to whom the Incarnation of Christ,
Thy Son, was made known by the message of an angel,
may by His Passion and Cross be brought to the glory of His
Resurrection.
Through the same Christ our Lord.

℟. Amen.

℣. Glory be to the Father, and to the Son, and to the Holy Spirit.

℟. As it was in the beginning, is now and ever shall be, world without end.

Amen.

Regina Caeli

Queen of heaven, rejoice, alleluia.
The Son you merited to bear, alleluia,
Has risen as he said, alleluia.
Pray to God for us, alleluia.
℣. Rejoice and be glad, O Virgin Mary, alleluia.
℟. For the Lord has truly risen, alleluia.
Let us pray. O God, who have been pleased
to gladden the world by the Resurrection

of your Son our Lord Jesus Christ,
grant, we pray, that through his Mother,
the Virgin Mary, we may receive the joys
of everlasting life. Through Christ our Lord. ℟. Amen.

O Sacrament Most Holy

O Sacrament most Holy,
O Sacrament Divine,
All praise and all thanksgiving,
Be every moment Thine.

Prayer to Jesus, Mary, and Joseph

Jesus, Mary, and Joseph, I give you my heart and my soul;
Jesus, Mary, and Joseph help me when I am dying;
Jesus, Mary, and Joseph may I breathe forth my spirit in peace with
you.
Amen

O My Jesus

O my Jesus,
forgive us our sins,
save us from the fire of hell,
lead all souls to heaven,
especially those who are in most need of Thy mercy.

Prayer of Sacrifice

Lord of the Holy Sacrifice, your saving oblation on the cross has given me new life.

May I always recall your holy sacrifice on the cross and do it in remembrance of you.

When tempted by selfishness,

inspire me to be taken as an unworthy sacrifice.

When burdened by envy,
let me become an instrument of blessing for others.
When afflicted by anger and pride,
grant me the humility to be broken and given for others.
When unsettled by anguish and troubled by worries,
give me encouragement.

May your Spirit move my heart to see in your outstretched arms your loving embrace of everyone that I, too, may welcome others with the same love in an open hand.
Teach my mind and direct my will to humbly endure the pain of undeserved suffering even when my intent was good and done what is right.
May I understand that it is in the holy sacrifice of your wounds that my brokenness is healed.
May I see in your sacrifice on the cross not only death and defeat but victory and life.
Loving Father, may the holy sacrifice of your Son cleanse my soul,

strengthen my heart, pardon my past and restore me in your peace.

May I always adore you by uniting myself in His holy sacrifice, the sacrament of your divine love.
May I learn to sacrifice my own comfort, plans, and dreams if it is not for your glory and the good of others.

With Mary, the mother of Jesus, who joined her heart with the sacrifice of her Son, may I become a holy sacrifice of love and service for others.
Gathered around the altar of love, may all be united in listening to your word and sharing the one bread and cup and become one people, offering one holy sacrifice.

Amen.

POWERFUL PRAYERS

Pray using the following powerful Prayers when facing extra-ordinary circumstancies. Pray them from the soul, slowly and meaningfully.

The golden arrow

May the most holy,

most sacred, most adorable,

most mysterious and unutterable Name of God

be always praised, blessed, loved, adored, and glorified

in heaven on earth and under the earth,

by all the creatures of God,

and by the Sacred Heart of our Lord Jesus Christ

in the Most Holy Sacrament of the altar.

Powerful prayer to the infant Jesus

O Child Jesus, I have recourse to You

through Your Holy Mother;

I implore You to assist me in this necessity,

for I firmly believe that Your Divinity can assist me.

I confidently hope to obtain Your holy grace.

I love You with my whole heart and my whole soul.

I am heartily sorry for my sins, and entreat You,

O good Jesus, to give me strength to overcome them.

I am firmly resolved never to offend You

again and to suffer everything rather

than displease You.

Henceforth, I wish to serve You faithfully.

For love of You, O divine Child,

I will love my neighbor as myself.

O Jesus, omnipotent Child,

I entreat You again to come to my assistance in this necessity. [Mention it here].

Grant me the grace of possessing You eternally

with Mary and Joseph and of adoring You

with Your Holy Angels and Saints. Amen.

Powerful Novena to the Sacred Heart

Glory be to the Father

Sacred Heart of Jesus,

I place all my trust in you,

and grant us the grace which we ask of You,

through the Sorrowful and Immaculate Heart of Mary,

Your tender mother and ours.

May this Novena to the Sacred Heart

bring you closer to the Heart of our Lord!

Amen

INTERCESSORY PRAYERS

The doctrine of asking intercession from the Saints is found on the early years of Christianism. Use the following prayers to claim exhortation and to elevate your devotion.

*Novena Prayer to Our Lady
of Good Remedy*

O QUEEN OF HEAVEN AND EARTH,

Most Holy Virgin, we venerate thee.

Thou art the beloved Daughter of the Most High God,

the chosen Mother of the Incarnate Word,

the Immaculate Spouse of the Holy Spirit,

the Sacred Vessel of the Most Holy Trinity.

O Mother of the Divine Redeemer,

who under the title of Our Lady of Good Remedy

comes to the aid of all who call upon thee,

extend thy maternal protection to us.

We depend on thee, Dear Mother,

as helpless and needy children depend

on a tender and caring mother.

Hail, Mary

O LADY OF GOOD REMEDY,

source of unfailing help,

grant that we may draw from thy treasury
of graces in our time of need.
Touch the hearts of sinners,
that they may seek reconciliation and forgiveness.
Bring comfort to the afflicted and the lonely;
help the poor and the hopeless;
aid the sick and the suffering.
May they be healed in body and strengthened
in spirit to endure their sufferings
with patient resignation and Christian fortitude.

Hail, Mary

DEAR LADY OF GOOD REMEDY,
source of unfailing help,
thy compassionate heart knows
a remedy for every affliction
and misery we encounter in life.
Help me with thy prayers and intercession
to find a remedy for my problems and needs,
especially for...
(Indicate your special intentions here).
On my part, O loving Mother,
I pledge myself to a more intensely Christian lifestyle,
to a more careful observance of the laws of God,
to be more conscientious in fulfilling the obligations of my state in
life, and to strive to be a source
of healing in this broken world of ours.
Dear Lady of Good Remedy,
be ever-present to me,

and through thy intercession,
may I enjoy health of body and peace of mind,
and grow stronger in the faith
and in the love of thy Son, Jesus.

Hail, Mary

V. Pray for us, O Holy Mother of Good Remedy,
R. That we may deepen our dedication to thy Son,
and make the world alive with His Spirit.

Prayer to Saint Joseph

O Saint Joseph,
O assist me by your powerful intercession,
and obtain for me from your Divine Son
all spiritual blessings, through Jesus Christ, our Lord,
So that, having engaged here below your heavenly power,
I may offer my thanksgiving and homage
to the most Loving of Fathers.
Amen

Prayer to Saint Anne

O Glorious St. Ann, filled with compassion for those who invoke thee and with love for those who suffer, heavily laden with the weight of my troubles, I cast myself at thy feet and humbly beg of thee to take under thy

special protection the present affair which I commend to thee.
Amen

Prayer to Saint Jude

St. Jude, you are the patron of the impossible.
Pray for me and my intentions!
Pray that I may have the grace to accept God's holy
will even if it is painful and difficult for me
Amen

Prayer to Saint Anthony of Padua

Blessed be God in His Angels and in His Saints
O Holy St. Anthony, gentlest of Saints,
your love for God and Charity for His creatures,
made you worthy, when on earth,
to possess miraculous powers.
Encouraged by this thought, I implore you to obtain for me
[Mention your request here].
O gentle and loving St. Anthony,
whose heart was ever full of human sympathy,
whisper my petition into the ears of the sweet Infant Jesus,
who loved to be folded in your arms;
and the gratitude of my heart will ever be yours.
Amen.

Prayer to St Rita for the impossible

O Holy Patroness of those in need, St. Rita, whose pleadings before
thy Divine Lord are almost irresistible,
who for thy lavishness in granting favors hast been called the Advocate of the HOPELESS and even of the IMPOSSIBLE;

St. Rita, so humble, so pure, so mortified, so patient and of such compassionate love for the Crucified Jesus that thou couldst obtain from Him whatsoever thou askest, on account of which all confidently have recourse to thee, expecting,

if not always relief, at least comfort; be propitious to our petition, showing thy power with God on behalf of thy suppliant; be lavish to us, as thou hast been in so many wonderful cases, for the greater glory of God, for the spreading of thine own devotion, and for the consolation of those who trust in thee.

We promise, if our petition is granted, to glorify thee by making known thy favor, to bless and sing thy praises forever. Relying then upon thy merits and power before the Sacred Heart of Jesus, we pray thee grant that (here mention your request).

By the singular merits of thy childhood, obtain for us our request.

By thy perfect union with the Divine Will, obtain for us our request.

By thy heroic sufferings during thy married life, obtain for us our request.

By the consolation thou didst experience at the conversion of thy husband, obtain for us our request.

By the sacrifice of thy children rather than see them grievously offend God, obtain for us our request.

By the severe penances and thrice daily scourgings, obtain for us our request.

By the suffering caused by the wound thou didst receive from the thorn of thy Crucified Savior, obtain for us our request.

By the divine love which consumed thy heart, obtain for us our request.

By that remarkable devotion to the Blessed Sacrament, on which alone thou dost exist for four years, obtain for us our request.

CATHOLIC PRAYERS : BEAUTIFUL DEVOTIONS

By the happiness with which thou didst part from thy trials to join thy Divine Spouse, obtain for us our request.

By the perfect example, you gavest to people of every state of life, obtain for us our request.

Pray for us, O holy St. Rita, that we may be made worthy of the promises of Christ.

Let us pray:

O God, Who in Thine infinite tenderness hast vouchsafed to regard the prayer of Thy servant, Blessed Rita, and dost grant to her supplication that which is impossible to human foresight, skill and efforts, in reward of her compassionate love and firm reliance on Thy promise, have pity on our adversity and succor us in our calamities, that the unbeliever may know Thou art the recompense of the humble, the defense of the helpless, and the strength of those who trust in Thee, through Jesus Christ, Our Lord. Amen.

Prayer to All the Angels
for special request

Bless the Lord, all ye His Angels!
Thou who art mighty in strength and do His Will,
intercede for me at the throne of God.
By thine unceasing watchfulness,
protect me in every danger of soul and body.
Obtain for me the grace of final perseverance,
so that after this life, I may be admitted
to thy glorious company and sing with thee the praises of God for

all eternity.

All ye holy Angels and Archangels, Thrones and Dominations,

Principalities and Powers and Virtues of Heaven,

Cherubim and Seraphim, and especially thou,

my dear Guardian Angel, intercede for me and obtain for me the

special favor I now ask.

(Mention your Intention).

Amen

A Prayer for Priests

O Jesus, eternal Priest,

keep your priests within the shelter of Your Sacred Heart,

where none may touch them.

Keep unstained their anointed hands,

which daily touch Your Sacred Body.

Keep unsullied their lips,

daily purpled with your Precious Blood.

Keep pure and unearthly their hearts,

sealed with the sublime mark of the priesthood.

Let Your holy love surround them and

shield them from the world's contagion.

Bless their labors with abundant fruit and

may the souls to whom they minister be their joy

and consolation here and in heaven their beautiful and

everlasting crown.

Amen

Prayer to our Lady of Guadalupe

O Immaculate Virgin, Mother of the true God
and Mother of the Church!,
who from this place reveal your clemency
and your pity to all those who ask for
your protection, hear the prayer that
we address to you with filial trust,
and present it to your Son Jesus,
our sole Redeemer.
Mother of Mercy,
Teacher of hidden and silent sacrifice,
to you, who come to meet us, sinners,
we dedicate on this day all our being
and all our love.
We also dedicate to you
our life, our work, our joys, our infirmities
and our sorrows.
Grant peace, justice
and prosperity to our peoples;
for we entrust
to your care all that we have and all
that we are, our Lady and Mother.
We wish to be entirely yours and
to walk with you along the way of complete
faithfulness to Jesus Christ in His Church;
hold us always with your loving hand.
Virgin of Guadalupe, Mother of the Americas,
we pray to you for all the Bishops,

that they may lead the faithful along
paths of the intense Christian life, of love
and humble service of God and souls.
Contemplate this immense harvest,
and intercede with the Lord that
He may instill a hunger for holiness
in the whole people of God, and grant
abundant vocations of priests and religious,
strong in the faith and zealous dispensers
of God's mysteries. Grant to our homes
the grace of loving and respecting life
in its beginnings, with the same love
with which you conceived in your
womb the life of the Son of God.
Blessed Virgin Mary, protect our families,
so that they may always be united,
and bless the upbringing of our children.
Our hope, look upon us with compassion,
teach us to go continually to Jesus and,
if we fall, help us to rise again, to return to Him,
by means of the confession of our faults
and sins in the Sacrament of Penance,
which gives peace to the soul.
We beg you to grant us a great love
for all the holy Sacraments,
which are, as it were, the signs that your Son
left us on earth.
Thus, Most Holy Mother,
with the peace of God in our conscience,
with our hearts free from evil and hatred,

we will be able to bring to all true joy
and true peace, which comes to us from your son,
our Lord Jesus Christ,
who with God the Father
and the Holy Spirit lives
and reigns forever and ever.
Amen

A prayer for Grace

Help me O God, because,
like all the children of men,
I need your daily grace.
Yesterday's blessings can encourage
but will not take care of the burdens of today.
May I know Thee as the Shepherd of my life
and eternal soul.
May my fears be dissolved
by faith in Thee and through the power of Thy love.
Help me to love and manifest the spirit of love
under all circumstances to all people.
May my life be a glory to Thyself,
a help to my fellow-man
and rewarding to me.
In Jesus' name,
Amen.

Prayer to Saint Gabriel, Archangel

Blessed Saint Gabriel, Archangel,

we beseech you to intercede for us at the throne of divine mercy.

As you announced the mystery of the Incarnation to Mary, so through your prayers may we receive strength of faith and courage of spirit, and thus find favor with God and redemption through Christ Our Lord.

May we sing the praise of God our Savior with the angels and saints in heaven forever and ever.
Amen.

Archangel St. Gabriel, pray for us!
Amen

God, Who Are You?

Almighty Creator of all what is seen and unseen,
Who are You?
Are you the God of my family tradition, the only God known to me?
Are you the God of Abraham, the God of the Jews?
Are you Muhammad, Buddha, Allah or one of the Hindu gods?
How does one get to know you if you will not reveal yourself?
How can one learn about you or your teachings if you remain hidden?
How can one find the way to eternal happiness if your remain mysterious?
How can one learn good or evil without a teacher?
How can you condemn the actions of one who is not guided in your way?

God, who are you? How long must you remain a mystery in my life?

Reveal yourself so I may know you and follow you.

Please, I beg you, tell me who you are.

Prayer To God The Father

Eternal Father,
I offer unto Thee the infinite satisfaction
which Jesus rendered to Thy justice
on behalf of sinners upon the tree of the Cross;
and I pray that Thou wouldst make the merits of His Precious
Blood available to all guilty souls
to whom sin has brought death;
may they rise again to the life of grace
and glorify Thee for ever.

Eternal Father,
I offer Thee the fervent devotion of the Sacred Heart of Jesus
in satisfaction for the lukewarmness and cowardice of Thy chosen
people,
imploring Thee by the burning love
which made Him suffer death,
that it may please Thee to rekindle their hearts
now so lukewarm in Thy service,
and to set them on fire with Thy love,
that they may love Thee for ever.

Eternal Father,
I offer Thee the submission of Jesus to Thy will,

and I ask of Thee,
through His merits,
the fullness of all grace
and the accomplishment of all Thy holy will.
Blessed be God!
Amen

The Prayer God's Will

Dear Lord God Almighty
We know that You are Jesus,
and that You died for us.
Give us Your Holy Spirit,
to live in us forever,
and thus bless us with eternal life.
Let Your Holy Spirit Testify through us
and speak the Truth through us.
Let Your Holy Spirit Love through us,
a perfect unselfish Holy Love;
so that we lay down all worldly ambitions,
give up our wills,
and do Your Holy Will.
Take our thoughts away from making money,
or finding business opportunities.
Take our desire away from seeking worldly wealth or fame.
Take our eyes away from looking on vain worldly appearances,
which deceive and mislead us.
Keep our thoughts on doing Your Holy will,
not on seeking worldly material things,

or vain worldly status.

Let Your Holy Spirit give us our one desire and one purpose,

To do Your Holy Will.

If You desire us to walk paths of poverty,

then so be it.

If You desire us to lose everything,

that we think is important or valuable,

then so be it.

If You desire us to sacrifice everything we have and our lives,

then so be it.

If You desire us to endure pain and seasons of harsh conditions,

then so be it.

If You desire us to live or die,

then so be it.

Let Your Holy Will be done in our lives.

For, even our lives are not our own.

We owe everything to You.

Keep us from looking in the mirror

and admiring our own beauty,

which is not beauty at all.

Let the True Beauty that is in us

Be Your Holy Spirit of Truth and Grace.

Keep us from pride and love of self,

which is our enemy.

Bless us with absolute, total, unselfish Love.

Which is only possible through Your Holy Spirit.

We give You our lives,

Do with us as You Will.

Make our lives useful to Your Service.

The only ambition we have is to humbly,
and honestly do Your Will.
We want to lift up Your Name Jesus,
not our names.
We want to make known the power of Your Holy Spirit, Jesus
We want You to claim us for Yourself,
and use us according to Your Divine purpose.
And no matter the job or task that You assign to us,
we will be contented,
and full of Joy,
to do Your Holy Will, Jesus.

Let Your Holy Spirit, Jesus,
Live in us forever,
and give us Purpose, Hope,
and Peace and Joy, and Eternal Life.
For without You, we perish.
In Your Holy Spirit, Jesus, we Pray!
Amen.

THE COMMUNION

Prayer before Communion

O Lord, I am not worthy that Thou should come under the roof of my house, for I am sinful, but say Thou first a word and my soul shall be healed.

Say unto my soul: "Your sins are forgiven." I am barren and wanting all righteousness, and have but Thy compassion, mercy and Love-of-Man.

And Thou hast condescended from the heaven of Thine ineffable glory to our afflictions and accepted to be born in a manger.

Reject not, O my blessed Saviour to come into my lowly and afflicted soul that awaits Thy radiant presence. But accept to come into my soul to cleanse it.

O Thou who disdained not to enter into the leper's house and to heal him, forbid me not to approach Thy pure Body and Thy Holy Blood, O Thou who prevented not the woman, who was a sinner, from kissing they feet.

Let my communion be for partaking with Thee and for effacing all defilement, the mortification of my lusts, the doing of Thy Life-giving commandments, the healing of my soul and body from all sins, the acceptance of Thy gifts, the endwelling of Thy grace, the descent of Thy spirit for union with and abiding in Thee, that I may live for the glory of Thy Holy Name.

Amen.

Prayer after the communion

I thank You, O holy Lord, almighty Father, eternal God, who have deigned, not through any merits of mine, but out of the condescension of Your goodness, to satisfy me a sinner, Your unworthy servant, with the precious Body and Blood of Your Son, our Lord Jesus Christ.

I pray that this Holy Communion be not a condemnation to punishment for me, but a saving plea to forgiveness.

May it be to me the armor of faith and the shield of a good will. May it be the emptying out of my vices and the extinction of all lustful desires; and increase of charity and patience, of humility and obedience, and all virtues; a strong defense against the snares of all my enemies, visible and invisible; the perfect quieting of all my evil impulses of flesh and spirit, binding me firmly to You, the one true God;

and a happy ending of my life.

I pray too that You will deign to bring me, a sinner,

to that ineffable banquet where You with Your Son and the Holy Spirit, are to your Saints true light, fulfillment of desires, eternal joy, unalloyed gladness, and perfect bliss.

Through the same Christ our Lord.
Amen.

CONFESSION PRAYERS

Preparation to confession prayer

My God, I am sorry for my sins with all my heart.
In choosing to do wrong and failing to do what is good,
I have sinned against You whom I should love above all things,
I firmly intend, with Your help, to do penance, to sin no more, and
to avoid whatever leads me to sin.
Our Savior Jesus Christ, suffered and died for us.
In His name, my God, have mercy.
Amen.

Prayer before the confession

Receive my confession, O most loving and gracious Lord Jesus
Christ, only hope for the salvation of my soul.

Grant to me true contrition of soul, so that day and night I may by
penance make satisfaction for my many sins. Savior of the world,
O good Jesus, Who gave Yourself to the death of the Cross to save
sinners, look upon me, most wretched of all sinners; have pity on
me, and give me the light to know my sins, true sorrow for them,
and a firm purpose of never committing them again.

O gracious Virgin Mary, Immaculate Mother of Jesus, I implore you to obtain for me by your powerful intercession these graces from your Divine Son.

St. Joseph, pray for me.

I confess

I confess to almighty God
and to you, my brothers,
that I have greatly sinned,
in my thoughts and in my words,
in what I have done and in what I have failed to do,
through my fault, through my fault,
through my most grievous fault;
therefore I ask blessed Mary ever-Virgin,
all the Angels and Saints,
and you, my brothers,
to pray for me to the Lord our God.

Prayer after confession

O almighty and most merciful God,

I give You thanks with all the powers of my soul for this and all other mercies, graces, and blessings bestowed on me, and prostrating myself at Your sacred feet, I offer myself to be henceforth forever Yours.

Let nothing in life or death ever separate me from You! I renounce

with my whole soul all my treasons against You, and all the abominations and sins of my past life.

I renew my promises made in Baptism, and from this moment I dedicate myself eternally to Your love and service.

Grant that for the time to come, I may detest sin more than death itself, and avoid all such occasions and companies as have unhappily brought me to it.

This I resolve to do by the aid of Your divine grace, without which I can do nothing.

Amen.

PRAYERS FROM THE PSALMS

A prayer to ask the Lord to help us walk with Him

Psalm 119:33-40

Lord, teach me the way of your statutes,
And I will keep them to the end.
Grant me insight that I may keep your law,
And observe it wholeheartedly.
Guide me in the path of your commands,
For in them is my delight.
Bend my heart to your decrees,
And not to wrongful gain.
Turn my eyes from gazing on vanities;
In your way, give me life.
Fulfill your promise to your servant,
That you may be revered.
Turn away the taunts I dread,
For your decrees are good.
See, I long for your precepts;
Give me life by your righteousness.

A prayer of thanksgiving and praise
(that promises to proclaim God's goodness to all generations)

Psalm 71:17-22

O God, you have taught me from my youth,

And I proclaim your wonders still.

Even till I am old and gray-headed,

Do not forsake me, O God.

Let me tell of your mighty arm

To every coming generation;

Your strength and your justice, O God,

Reach to the highest heavens.

It is you who have worked such wonders.

O God, who is like you?

You have made me witness many troubles and evils,

But you will give me back my life.

You will raise me from the depths of the earth;

You will exalt me and console me again.

So I will give you thanks of the lyre

For your faithfulness, O my God.

To you will I sing with the harp,

To you, the Holy One of Israel.

A prayer of total worship and adoration of God
(a prayer that invites others to do the same)

Psalm 148:1-2, 11-14

Alleluia!

Praise the Lord from the heavens;

Praise the Lord in the heights

Praise the Lord, all his angels;

Praise the Lord, all his hosts.

Rulers of the earth and all peoples,

Sovereigns and all judges of the earth,

Young men and maidens as well,

The old and the young together.

Let them praise the name of the Lord,

For God's name alone is exalted,

Whose splendor rises above heaven and earth.

The Lord exalts the strength of the people,

And is the praise of all the faithful

The praise of the children of Israel,

Of the people to whom our God is close.

Alleluia!

A quiet, intimate prayer between the reader and God

Psalm 63:1-8

You, God, are my God,

I earnestly seek you;

I thirst for you,

My whole being longs for you,

In a dry and parched land

Where there is no water.
I have seen you in the sanctuary
And beheld your power and your glory.
Because your love is better than life,
My lips will glorify you.
I will praise you as long as I live,
And in your name I will lift up my hands.
I will be fully satisfied with the richest of foods;
With singing lips my mouth will praise you.
On my bed, I remember you;
I think of you through the watches of the night.
Because you are my help,
I sing in the shadow of your wings.
I cling to you;
Your right hand upholds me.

Psalm 16:5,8

"Lord, you alone are my portion and my cup;
you make my lot secure.
I keep my eyes always on the Lord.
With him at my right hand,
I will not be shaken."

Psalm 27:10

"Though my father and mother forsake me,
the Lord will receive me."

Psalm 91:2,4

"I will say of the Lord,

"He is my refuge and my fortress,

my God, in whom I trust.

He will cover you with his feathers, and under his wings you will

find refuge; his faithfulness will be your shield and rampart."

Psalm 34:1-3

"I will extol the Lord at all times;

his praise will always be on my lips.

I will glory in the Lord;

let the afflicted hear and rejoice.

Glorify the Lord with me;

let us exalt his name together."

Psalm 142:1-2

"I cry aloud to the Lord;

I lift up my voice to the Lord for mercy.

I pour out before him my complaint;

before him I tell my trouble."

Psalm 37:3-4, 7

"Trust in the Lord and do good;

dwell in the land and enjoy safe pasture.

Take delight in the Lord,

and he will give you the desires of your heart.

Be still before the Lord and wait patiently for him;

do not fret when people succeed in their ways,

when they carry out their wicked schemes."

A modern prayer if you're worried
about the COVID19 pandemic
(or any other difficult trial facing our times today)

Psalm 46:2-4, 9-12

God is for us a refuge and strength,

An ever-present help in time of distress:

So we shall not fear though the earth should rock,

Though the mountains quake to the heart of the sea;

Even though its waters rage and foam,

Even though the mountains be shaken by its tumult.

The Lord of hosts is with us:

The God of Jacob is our stronghold.

Come and behold the works of the Lord,

The awesome deeds God has done on the earth.

God puts an end to wars all over the earth;

Breaking bows, snapping spears, and burning shields with fire:

"Be still and know that I am God,

Exalted over nations, exalted over Earth!"

The Lord of hosts is with us:

The God of Jacob is our stronghold.

PRAYERS FOR SPECIFIC NEEDS

Prayer to overcome anxiety

Loving God, please grant me peace of mind
and calm my troubled heart.
My soul is like a turbulent sea.
I can't seem to find my balance
so I stumble and worry constantly.
Give me the strength and clarity of mind
to find my purpose
and walk the path you've laid out for me.

Prayer for hope

Heavenly father, I am your humble servant,
I come before you today in need of hope.
There are times when I feel helpless,
There are times when I feel weak.
I pray for hope.
I need hope for a better future.
I need hope for a better life.
I need hope for love and kindness.
Some say that the sky is at it's

darkest just before the light.
I pray that this is true, for all seems dark.
I need your light, Lord, in every way.
I pray to be filled with your light from
head to toe. To bask in your glory.
To know that all is right in the world,
as you have planned, and as you want
it to be.
Help me to walk in your light, and live
my life in faith and glory.
In your name I pray, Amen.

Prayer for better sleep

Now I lay down to sleep,
I pray to you, the Lord my soul to keep,
watch and guard me through the night,
and wake me with the morning light.
Almighty God, radiant with light,
cast your goodness to shine upon me.
Most wonderful Lord,
creator of all things,
hold your truth to shield me.
Amen

Prayer for couples

God of Unfailing Love, may we be filled with love for each other that reflects your love for us.

Your love is patient, let us be patient with each other.

Your love is kind, let us be kind to each other.

Your love does not envy, let us not be envious of each other.

Your love does not boast, may our relationship be built on humility.

You love does not dishonor others, let us honor each other.

Your love is not self-seeking, let us love each other with a selfless love.

Help us to love each other well.

Through Jesus Christ, our Lord, Amen.

Prayer for friends

Loving Father,
I want to thank You for giving me the wonderful circle of friends that I have.
You have surrounded me with people that really love You and that want to know me more each day!
Thank you, Lord, for they have all shown me so much love and I am truly grateful for their friendship.
Thank you for providing me with friends that hold me accountable in my walk with You as I hold them accountable as well.
Lord, I praise Your holy name for blessing me with such amazing friends! I love You, Father!
Amen

Prayer for leadership

Oh Lord, Your Word declares that You are our Good Shepherd. Just as shepherds provides guidance for their sheep, we pray that You, Lord, provide guidance for every leader.

I pray that You help them to be more like You.

Help them know the condition of their flock.

I pray that every leader gives careful attention those they lead, and that the relationship between those they lead will flourish.

This is the prayer of our heart.

Amen.

Prayer for better finances

O Father
You are the God of all resources.
Everything is at your disposal.
Life is tough right now and money is even tighter.
I need your provision to help me take care of all that needs to be taken care of in my life.
Please come to my rescue and quickly,
I'm drowning.

Amen.

Prayer for overcoming depression

O God,

I cry out to You Lift my eyes to see hope rise.

I cry out to You Change the colour of my thoughts to a sunny day.

I cry out to You Blow away the dark clouds to bring Your light.

I cry out to You Break into my heavy heart and breathe Your life into me.

That in the morning I may rise to a shinny day,

full of Your light and breathing Your life.

Lord, I cry out to You.

Amen.

Prayer for wisdom

God, give me wisdom to accept with calm
the things that cannot be changed,
Courage to change the things
which should be changed at your desire,
and the discerment to distinguish
the one from the other.
Living one day at a time,
Lord, give me the Grace
to enjoy one moment at a time,
Accepting this hardship as a pathway to peace,
Taking, as your son Jesus did,
This sinful world as it is,
Not as I would have it,
Trusting that You will make all things right,
If I surrender to Your will,
So that I may be reasonably happy in this life,
And supremely happy with You forever in the next.

Amen.

Restoring Prayer

O Lord,

drive away from me all forms of sickness and disease.
restore strength to my body and joy to my spirit,
so that in my renewed health,
I may bless and serve you,
now and forevermore.

Amen

❖ ❖ ❖

INDEX

Alphabetical list of prayers

I confess

Joyful Mysteries

Luminous Mysteries

Memorare

Morning Offering

Morning Prayer

Night Prayer

Novena Prayer to Our Lady of Good Remedy

O My Jesus

O Sacrament Most Holy

Our Father

Powerful Novena to the Sacred Heart

Powerful prayer to the infant Jesus

Prayer after confession

Prayer after the communion

Prayer After the Rosary

Prayer before Communion

Prayer before the confession

Prayer for Acceptance of Death

Prayer for better finances

Prayer for better sleep

Prayer for couples

Prayer for friends

Prayer for hope

Prayer for leadership

Prayer for overcoming depression

Prayer for wisdom

Prayer of Sacrifice

Prayer to All the Angels for special request

Prayer To God The Father

Prayer to Jesus, Mary, and Joseph

Prayer to our Lady of Guadalupe

Prayer to overcome anxiety

Prayer to Saint Anne

Prayer to Saint Anthony of Padua

Prayer to Saint Gabriel, Archangel

Prayer to Saint Joseph

Prayer to Saint Jude

Prayer to St Rita for the impossible

Prayer to the archangel Saint Michael

Preparation to confession prayer

Regina Caeli

Restoring Prayer

Sacred Heart of Jesus Prayer

Sign of the Cross

Sorrowful Mysteries

Thanksgiving After Meals

The Angelus

The Apostle's Creed

The Divine Praises

The golden arrow

The Prayer God's Will

THE LAST WORD

In this book, I compiled some of the most beautiful and touching catholic prayers, to enhance the connection between you and God.

These prayers, aspirations and hymns have emerged from the story of the Church in various times and places and have become an integral part of the ongoing prayer life of the Church. They are now part of popular culture, bringing peace of mind to thousands and thousands of good Christians, as yourself.

Let Prayers unify all us, Catholic people, around the message of love from Jesus; prayers will promote communion with God and will increase the knowledge of God's word.

As Catholics, We are asked to spread the joy of Prayers accros the community. If this book made you any good, please share your comments and leave a review on Amazon.

God bless you!

BOOKS BY THIS AUTHOR

Prayer Exercises For The Elderly

Pocket Prayers for Calm is a guide through 55 prayers to help you go through your life with calm and joy.

Devocionario Católico

Spanish complete devocional book
Todo católico debiera tener esta libro de devociones entre otras, para honrar la obra del Padre todopoderoso.
En este devocionario, usted encontrara oraciones para todos los momentos del día.

The Short Guide To Practicing Meditation

Mindful living is about living with awareness in the present moment. Mindful living meaning involves taking care of your actions, words, and feelings to ensure that you live a good and present life.
Transcendental meditation can change a life, going from being empty to living fully, placing your intentions, and being able to express your goals in life.
Use this guide for your meditative and observation practices. Practice manifestation of your goals, by setting up a routine of daily prayers and meditations.